Step Into My World

Poetry & Prose
by
Brian Beveridge

ACKNOWLEDGEMENTS

My thanks go to Nicky Beveridge for her delightful illustration and design of the front cover.

Thanks also go to Maggie's Expressive Writing Group, to which I belong. The ideas for some of the items included in this book originated from discussions and jottings in various of our meetings.

Furthermore I would like to pay tribute to my charming Polish friend, Jakub Raszteborski who so patiently and calmly transcribed my jottings and scribblings into a form that my printers were happy to accept.

The Family Chiropody Practice (www.chiropodypractice.com) kindly sponsored this publication and for this I am deeply grateful

---

Copies of this book may be obtained by emailing:
bribev893@tiscali.co.uk
or by telephoning

Pamela: 01463 798447

Profits from the sale of this book will be shared by Munlochy Animal Aid and Cats Protection.

CONTENTS

INDEX

Printer’s Error;

There is a minor misprint on the second page of the index. ‘Ponderings’ should be noted as Page 61, ‘If at First You Don’t Succeed’ should be noted as pages.62/63.

As Was ; 0-6 years

From an age of three score years and ten
I mind the times of why and when
of where and how and what and who
when all the world was large and new,
when parents seemed so big and tall
whilst I was rather thin and small.

Then Summer suns shone hot and long
from skies alive with the skylark's song
above the fields where mushrooms grew
and hedgerows gleamed with morning dew,
when days were full of wondrous sights
and the world was kindly, fresh and bright.
I'd run to meet the milkman's horse
with sugar lumps to cheer his course;
the garden swing would lift me high
to let me see the folk nearby
who oft would wave and give a smile
and pause to watch me for a while.

I doubt that now the shed still stands –
my vantage point o'er distant lands
where pirates dwelt and lived their lives
or tribesmen flourished wicked knives.
Beneath the chestnut tree it stood
to shade my daring Robin Hood.
But when imagination palled,
other pastimes always called.
I'd take my kite onto the Rye
and do my best to make it fly,
or hunt for snails and trap the slugs
then spray the flower killing bugs.

Some days I'd stand with raptured gaze
and watch the tramcars clank their ways.
It was such times I longed to rove
to find some secret treasure trove
until I lost the urge to stray
and found some other game to play.
A genie with his magic wand
would whisk me to the boating pond
or speed me to the local shop
to study sweets with eyes a-pop
'til I would run with flying feet
'Cos hunger drove me home to eat.

No love had I for greens or spam.
but always space for bread and jam,
for liquorice and bullseye sweets,
for strawberry ice cream - such a treat
if money spare there was to buy
reward for learning not to cry.
Thus through the childhood, forming years
I learnt to hold back welling tears.
'Be strong, my son, and do not yowl
for no-one likes a child who howls.'
Edwardian values still held strong
and sternly showed me right from wrong.

So thus my infant childhood ran
and shaped this rather aged man
who now recalls his early life
ere war brought change and pain and strife,
'til times that were became no more
and memories are 'days of yore'.

Awake, My Son

Awake, my son, you've much to learn
And even more to see.
Come, leave your cares behind you
and take the road with me.

Then you might see the mad March hares
a-boxing in the field,
the sexes battling forcefully
'til one or t'other yields.
You'll surely see the cream rumped deer
as they bound into the thicket
where safety lies for buck and doe
and many a growing pricket.

Then find the shaggy wild goat
as he peers from rocky crag-
so unafraid and curious-
with a stare that never flags.
Whilst overhead the fork-tailed kite
just cruises o'er the land
as finch and robin sing their songs
from hedgerows close at hand.

Would you awake to see the sun
enhance a snow-capped Ben
and hear a burn's soft rippling
on its journey to the glen
where lies a loch of plenty
just alive with rising fish
and to have a rod and fly to hand
becomes a fervent wish?

Awake, my son, you've much to learn
and even more to see.
Come, leave your cares behind you
and take the road with me.

I'll take you to Culloden's Moor
to grieve for slaughtered men
who lost their lives in'46
leaving empty croft and glen.
Now on this Moor the heather grows
and sheep do sometimes graze,
impervious to memories
that time cannot erase.

You've yet to know the tartan's swing
or be rallied by the call
of pipes that echo through the land –
they'll hold you in deep thrall.
As will Auld Reekie's Princes Street
or Orkney's Skara Brae
or Dornoch's wide and sweeping beach
and charming Castle Mey.

Sometimes we'll watch the night-time fall
as it sets the skies aflame
with colours vivid, bright and bold
so rose heads bow in shame.
'Tis then we'll join a ceilidh gay
and sing the songs of old;
we'll skip and dance to many a reel
and list to stories told.

Awake, my son, you've much to learn
and even more to see.
Come, leave your cares behind you
and take the road with me.

Then, as the night-time fades away
and dawn the day doth show,
we'll stroll the sands and clear our heads
of whisky's potent glow.
I'll show you these, and other things,
like berries from the cane,
fresh gathered on a Summer's morn
all swollen fat with rain.

Bere bannocks I will share with you
and we will gorge together
on Scotland's larder, rich and fine,
like grouse fresh shot from heather
or lobster, newly trapped at sea,
or lamb from Rogart's glen
and beef so flavoursome and sweet;
these you have yet to ken.

So whilst you lie there, fast asleep,
a youth on edge of man,
I fain would wake and take you off,
your heritage to span.
For you have yet so much to learn -
all lies within your grasp -
if you but dare to come with me,
your Homeland to enclasp.

Awake, my son, you've much to learn
And even more to see.
Come, leave your cares behind you
and take the road with me.

The Coal Fire's Glare

What dreams do you have, lying there
So sleepy in the coal fire's glare?

In daylight bright I've watched you run.
Across the fields 'neath blazing sun;
Down the paths and through the corn
Seeking – what? – on a Summer's morn.
Nose to ground when scent was strong,
You've hunted.gaily, carefree, long.
Now resting, coat as black as night,
So sleepy in the fire's light,
I wonder, do you long to be
Out in the country running free?

Or, as you tremble in your sleep,
Is it to be by rivers deep
Where splashing through the reeds and muck
You might flush out a brace of duck?
Or would you be on hills of shale
Where eagerly you've chased the quail
And where you've pounced on rabbits fat
And careless in their habitat?
Are these the scenes you long to know
When basking in the fire's glow?

But as you lie there, lithe and dark,
Perhaps you'd rather prance the park
And madly romp among the leaves
That, fallen, lie beneath the trees?
Or do your dreams turn to the strand
Where you could bound along the sand
And, barking, plunge into the race,
Retrieving sticks with easy grace
Before, once more, you stretch out there
So sleepy in the coal fire's glare?

Changes Are the Same

Bright orange dancing against a black background -
the coal fire is alive and well.
Black dog rests at its side,
absorbing warmth;
labrador's heavy head resting on extended legs.

And the fleeting picture is so familiar.

Yes, I've been here before …
penned a poem
from the heart.
But a different era. A different dog.

So little changes.

After Megan

What words are there that I can use
Now that you've gone from me?
I do suspect that there are none
To ease the misery
That permeates my heart and soul
And clouds my grieving mind
'Til I'm uncertain of my role
In the life you've left behind

For you are dead whilst I remain
Distressed and lost and low,
Receiver of impatient looks
From those who do not know
The life we shared, the love we had,
The bonds that held us tight;
Now memories are all I have
To take into the night

Of Life.

Just Another Day In the Week

Good Friday, visiting friends in Morayshire.

Their hillside farm, situated deep along the whisky trail, is a rolling, windswept series of fields all of which are open to the vagaries of the prevailing weather, whatever that may happen to be or have been.

This April Friday, the long track that snakes from the tarmacked road to the two storey house is a ribbon of potholes and melting snow which wickedly covers ice and frozen puddles.

My wife takes the car to the house. Happily abandoned I follow her on foot, together with our dogs. They need the exercise after the two hour drive to get here and I am ready for some fresh air.

Trudge. Trudge. Splash. Slower, more cautious movements through a particularly wet stretch of track, watching my step and seeing the dogs romp past huddled sheep and blanketed horses. Where, I wonder, are the few remaining pygmy goats that our friends keep? Probably inside their hut since they detest having wet feet and snow still coats the fields.

My attention has wavered and I pay the price. Skid. Stagger. Thump. Crash.

Prostrate and momentarily unaware of what has happened, I struggle to regain breath. As awareness percolates back, I see an interested and protective dog looming over my body and I feel her licking my face.

"What game is this, Daddy? Get up …."

No Good Friday this, but just another day with me sporting a sore shoulder, a grazed knee, a bruised hand and feeling very uncomfortable in cold and soaking wet clothing.

A disappointed dog accompanies me as I limp towards the house ….

And the Parrots Stare

Inverness; Autumn weather;
days sliding from wet Summer hours
to cold Winter winds
and snow on the Ben.

The central heating gurgles
and brings the parrots
a semblance of their homeland warmth.
But they stay on their perches
and stare dispassionately
at their surroundings.

How could it be otherwise?

Fashioned by an Italian craftsman's hands
they adorn the cabinets
from which they study silently
and uncomprehendingly
the world they are compelled
to inhabit

Perhaps they gaze in disbelief?

Contemplating the first stirrings of Spring

A dash of colour lures the eye
Amid the swath of green.
It holds one's glance enticingly
With a bursting, yellow sheen
That brightens long a Winter's day
And lifts the spirits high
So proudly does it cap the furze
To boldly prophesy
That gloomy, chilly, freezing days
Will soon make way for Spring.
The trees will leaf, the hedgerow bloom
And the countryside will sing.
So welcome, welcome first born flower
Atop the guarding thorns.
You bravely tell of days to come
When the land will be reborn
And Winter will be cast aside
To yield to season's clime
As spring revives a cheerless earth
And Summer bides her time.

From a leaf

I fell
Yet I did not so much fall as depart on a gentle wind which took me, swirling and gliding, from my summer home.
Now, in autumn, I lie amongst others, some of whom I know, and my world has taken on an entirely new perspective.
No longer do I flutter in the breeze or help shelter chirping birds. Instead I look up at those self same chaffinches and robins. But I still marvel at their songs as my colour alters and my strength wanes.
There is no doubt that I am changing, but my tree goes on...

From a tree

Letting go.
Denuded is the word that comes to mind
I am a great, burgeoning oak standing solidly by myself on the skyline of a rolling field. My huge branches are nakedly outlined by a winter sky. This is the result of letting go which, in itself, is part of the rhythm of the seasons.
Birth, life, growth and demise are all part of that progression and so my leaves were born and grew with me. They flourished and in their prime they gave me character and splendour. Now they have left me to go their own ways.
I miss them. Yet still I have beauty.

The West Wind's Song

The post van gentled 'long the track
Towards the lonely, quiet shack
Which housed The Ancients, old and frail,
Who dwelt there – held within the jail
That kept them still – despite their years
And gave them comfort, soothed their fears
Whilst age o'ertook them, eyes grew dim
As pain and stiffness gripped each limb
'Til they forgot the West Wind's song
That often whispered soft and strong
Around the broken eaves.

The fair West Wind that soughed its course
With gentle strength that stirred the gorse
So hedgerow danced as though to please
This Master kind that kissed the trees
And wafted sound to grazing deer
Who ceased their nibbling, pricked their ears,
Prepared to take to instant flight
If danger hove within their sight.
Yet 'twas not peril that they heard
But the keening cry of the hunting bird
That wheeled above their heads.

The West Wind's subtle, lifting draught
The buzzard rode as on a raft;
A gliding, circling, gazing ride
Which rabbits watched, prepared to hide
If once the stalking presence stooped
To scatter far the feeding group.

Thus through and round such rural sights
The soft wind passed, so warm and light,
To bless the fields and stir the clouds,
To coax the birds to sing out loud
From many a bush and tree.

And as this West Wind carolled on,
The sun came out and brightly shone
On copse and field, on hedgerow dense,
On rutted track and sagging fence;
It lightened up an ageing face
That peered out from the unkempt place
To which the post van lurched its way
En route, on such a Summer's day,
To hand the mail into the home
Where lived The Ancients, all alone,
Until their dying days.

Autumn Grey

Grey, misty, moisty, mellow morn
so peaceful, still and warm,
You wrap me in your Autumn cloak,
cocoon me with your calm.
I lean upon a sagging gate,
entranced by all I see –
the distant hills, the forest dark,
the hedgerow growing free
into the field where rabbits play
and sheep so often graze,
where cows will stand and chew the cud
on balmy Summer days.
Now, as your mist enfolds the hills,
a distant sound grows near
and a vocal skein of geese flies o'er,
unseen but calling clear;
whilst, far below, a hunting hawk
skims swiftly to the wood
where brambled paths make access hard
and a working croft once stood.
But that had been in days long past,
times seldom brought to mind,
so I turn away, forsake the gate,
and leave the past behind.
Before me winds the twisting track
through pines so tall and sheer
that nonetheless are Haven Safe
to marten, badger, deer,
and as I stroll so lazily
beneath the dripping trees,
some misty droplets coat my face,
propelled by a zephyr breeze
that whispers through the branches high
to stir the Autumn grey

and I feel content that I am here
to relish such a day.
But fleeting is my world of peace
and silence slips away;
there comes a fusillade of shots
resounding from the brae.
The guns are out to fill the pots
so pheasant, grouse beware,
Since quietude no longer reigns
and turmoil fills the air.
Grey, misty, moisty, mellow morn,
once peaceful, still and warm,
You wrapped me in your Autumn cloak
And blessed me with your calm.

Winter's Gift to the City

Birdlike, the kite flutters lazily in the still, wintry air,
striving to rise smoothly into the windless sky.
Conversely, the Beach Boys sing of sun, sand and life without care
far, far away from every new, excited cry
that rises sharply from the snowbound slopes.
Winter's gift to the city.

Toboggans speed crazily down ice-ridden mounds of grass
as empty cars sit monstrous, frozen and silent,
unused – unusable – in the cold winter's sun
which glints brightly off the hard packed roads
and trees bent heavily and laden with snow,
Winter's gift to the city.

The grubby, salt-spattered Corporation bus crammed with people
Visiting, working, afraid to drive in Winter's grip
edges past the silent church and lofty steeple
as tingling fingers lift to touch a frozen lip
and searching dogs sniff urgently at yellow stained snow.
Winter's gift to the city.

A red, nut filled net hangs cheerfully on the gaunt, iced fence
as, in unwritten code, the birds queue patiently
for sustenance whilst uncaring wains and parents
in their red, green, yellow and blue anoraks cluster intently
and gaily at the top of the toboggan slopes.
Winter's gift to the city.

And in the Victorian tenement blocks that overlook
the bright, white, noisy, below freezing open space
the wheezing and arthritic nurse The Good Book
and huddle defensively before their one saving grace,
the ancient gas fire which is their sole shield against
Winter's gift to the City.

Ode to a Pair

Of?

Suggestive subject, prone to make youths snigger
and young girls either blush coyly or breath more deeply.

But not so – not in the context of this exercise.

Swaying slightly, plump and rounded
and pretty to see.
So well outlined and attractive,
they exude fulfilment and good health,
and they draw the eye to their form.

A fine pair indeed.

Those two pigeons, resting on the branch
above my head.

For Horace ….

This poem is dedicated to Horace Dobbs, author, lecturer, dolphin expert and friend

The slithering, sinuous, smooth flowing sea
Stretched just as far as my keen eyes could see.
It hid all its dwellers well out of my sight
And nowt did I spot from the morn 'til the night.
With binoculars sharp did I scan every wave,
But nothing emerged from that watery grave;
No albatross followed our ship on its way
And only one puffin flew skittering away.
The Captain called, 'whales – there on the port bow'-
His eyesight was better than mine, I know now,
For some nearly seen whales did not brighten my day
And neither did porpoise come leaping to play.
I felt rather sad – and distinctly ignored;
To tell the truth, I was really quite bored.
All day did I watch, from morn 'til the eve,
Yet nothing transpired my gaze to relieve.
I hoped for some elk, or bears, on the strand,
Or even a walrus asleep on the sand.
The reindeer and foxes stayed well out of view
And this wildlife voyage I started to rue.
Then, suddenly, gracefully, from out of the deep
Some dolphins came bursting and started to leap.
The near setting sun cast its glow and enhanced
The joy and the fun of their frolicking dance
As they jumped and they chased and they dived in great style,
Their antics I watched and I felt myself smile,
My boredom now vanished, my sadness dispelled
As these nimble performers cast their magical spell.
So thank you, sleek dolphins, for lightening my day,
May you always bring cheer as you pass on your way.

Ramblings of a Neurotic Mind

Two minutes ago snow slanted across the garden,
driven by a branch-shaking wind.
I sit, huddled before the live, dancing fire
feeling so guilty, because
I am sitting in front of the live, dancing fire
and am not walking the dogs.

The keeping of animals brings responsibilities.
This I know. But Philip McCann's sweet, sweet cornet
playing
over-rides as it soars and sails on the airwaves,
touching my soul, invoking memories,
holding me entranced and trapped in a cocoon
where the past invades, the present demands,
and emotive Jerusalem brings tears to my eyes.

That long, controlled, haunting last note
sears its way into my being
and is the catalyst for hauling buried
memories to the forefront of my mind
whilst dogs lie poised and ever ready
to destroy my bubble of recollection.

Oh, God. We're entertaining again tonight.
Cannot forever sit here and dwell in the past.
Have things to do. Yet weariness pervades;
everything is energy-sapping and a botheration,
as the snow eases, the fire glows
and the last of the whisky bottle beckons.

Is this sum total of seventy-plus years?
Momentary dissatisfaction holds sway,
but is soon banished by reality.
A rational mind and Bruch's Scottish Fantasy
replace McCann. Intensity lessens
and I come tumbling back to The Present.

The snow still falls; my word is white
and permeated only by lilting, dancing music.

The Here and Now Rule…O.K?

A pre-Dinner Toast to .... ?

Slender, so slender, yet strong,
you bring much pleasure into my life.

How I gaze at your shape,
not with longing. not with envy,
but certainly with admiration
and appreciation.

How you manage to attract others;
how they flock around you.
I am in awe
of the gratification
your submissive form
so generously provides.

Like me, your visitors
bask in the enjoyment
you so freely and proudly provide.
I raise my glass in tribute …

Bird feeder.

Let These Leaves

Lie where they are; sodden. Brown, slippery to walk on as they gradually decompose in Winter's cold and relentless grip – and Springtime's winds and showers of rain.

An essential part of nature, and a large factor in Nature's circle of life, they lie beneath my feet as I wander aimlessly among the parent trees observing the fat black slugs, the lazy worms and the dashing spiders that inhabit this disintegrating carpet of dampness on which I meander. Gradually and slowly these dwellers will assist in the dissolution of the leaves and the subsequent feeding of the parent trees.

Cannabalism in its mildest form? Perhaps, in its final stages.

But for now I am searching for a newly tumbled, dry leaf.

Why?

I know not. Perhaps to prove to myself that such a thing exists at this time of year; possibly as a symbol of resistance against the inevitability of my own incurable cancer; a whim to find such a leaf after the previous night's rainfall; or just for the sheer daftness of doing such a thing at all. All these should be considered as motivational possibilities.

Yet as these leaves lie, they have no interest in me or my
physical and mental condition. They have no voice to cry
and rail against invading enemies. They cannot change
their life-style and residence without the assistance of the
probing wind or the sweeping rain … and they must
therefore remain to fulfil a destined role.

And I suspect that my search will prove to be fruitless

On Cancer

Recollections?

I do not have too many and that seems somehow unexpected considering the hold that cancer has on the general population. Nearly every family we know has someone or other affected. Perhaps I have adopted an "ostrich" policy – to bury my head and consider other things rather than to dwell in thoughts of the past and of this killer that now has me in its sights.

Much more to my own way of thinking – nay, querying – is to ponder as to how large a part does coincidence play, if any?. My mind returns to this puzzle with great frequency because I happen to live in a property in which the three previous family occupants all lost their alpha male to cancer. How big a coincidence is that, I ask myself, considering that I am well in line to be the fourth? Over a span of some forty years at least, two husbands have died of lung cancer, the third of throat cancer and I have the prostate problem. I find that I am contemplating this enigma with ever burgeoning regularity and bizarre, sometimes almost whimsical, fancifulness. Might some as yet undiscovered and unconsidered force have some bearing on the subject? Ley lines, for instance? Or magnetic points? Is there something other than just cells and genes involved?

I cannot stop my mind from dancing capriciously around such notions.

Apart from this I have been lucky, I guess, in that I have had direct personal contact and involvement in only three cancer cases. Even so, years later, whenever any of these three come to mind, I am subject to surges of guilt and emotion beside which my own problems pale into insignificance..

My father, in his late sixties, contracted lung cancer which subsequently produced a secondary in the brain. Eventually he was a helpless child, unable to do anything for himself. Unaided and alone my mother cared for him until he died … a lingering, six month process. But I was shielded from most of this in as much as I was living and working four hundred miles away, I had a family, I ran a small business that depended to large extent on my presence and at the time I could ill afford to travel those eight hundred miles there and back.

In retrospect, I think I should have tried harder….

Years later, my best friend, a character I had known and enjoyed for sixty years, contracted a rare form of lung cancer. Again, distance, cost and, I suppose, an inability to be of much help other than as a morale booster and an emotional sounding board , prevented my being of much assistance to the situation – or to his wife who also happened to be a long-standing friend. They lived in Hertfordshire, I lived in Inverness, but by then my wife and I were operating a small and busy bed and breakfast establishment together with a small-holding that had several animals for which we had responsibility; goats for milk and meat, sheep for wool and meat and pigs for just about everything else. Not to mention the hens, ducks and geese.

Dilemma; which takes precedence – friends, guests or animals?

I'm quite positive that my friend would have understood. And said so; we were on the same wave-length for so many years, years which time and distance were unable to fracture and destroy. Nevertheless, I cannot but regret that I was of so little assistance. I felt helpless and annoyed when the finality of it all arrived. We had been good pals for such a long time and we had a very special relationship that was irreplaceable, but c'est la vie, I told myself; that era has finished so just get on with life. But that does not prevent my mourning his departure deeply and wishing, only too late, that I might somehow have been of better comfort and support to them in his fading years.

The third case was somewhat different … and surely has something to say about my mental and emotional priorities.

Bruce, a rather dopey, laid-back labrador/collie cross dog had been with us since birth. He was fun, an gentle, easy-going beast with, as was often stated, 'not a bad bone in his body'. We just loved this quiet, dependable animal that had somehow managed to insert himself into our lives, despite the much more overt and effervescent attentions of his companion pack. .But this seven year old dog, still in his prime, had been off colour, we noted, for a few days, so we took him to the vet.

We were devastated, a few days later, when were informed that he had cancer. We had never come across such a thing before, not in an animal, and the news was a great shock. This was in June and we were told that it was very unlikely he would see the coming Christmas. This proved to be very true and we had him put down on the last day of September. His decline had been swift and marked in the intervening few months. Prior to my own diagnosis this proved to be my one *close* contact with cancer.

Nonetheless, the illness and death of this dog had a long-lasting and emotional effect on my life, far more so than did those of my father and friend. Does that make me a shallow person, I wonder? A man whose priorities are off balance and in need of re-adjustment? I had no answer to these self-imposed questions.

Iit was but a short time after Bruce's demise, whilst I was still inwardly grieving his loss, that my own cancer was first diagnosed. 'Aggressive' the doctor called it in his earnest' I've- got- bad- news- for- you manner'. His pronouncement seemed not to take into account my previous explanations of symptoms that had been bothering me for more than a year and which he had failed to recognise other than to suggest that they were typical problems due to my age. In fact, it was the thoroughness of a German locum doctor that had first put me on the road to discovery of the cancer by an hospital consultant to whom he had referred me for examination.

A high psa count, a biopsy and a somewhat uncomfortable internal examination proved that I had developed prostate cancer and some form of interim treatment was necessary pending further examination and tests at the hospital. This was the news that a serious faced doctor imparted to me as I sat politely in his functional, rather dreary consulting room. But even as he spoke my thoughts drifted elsewhere; the Ley lines, or magnetic field, or whatever, had struck again was the first thought that rather facetiously invaded my mind, hotly followed by the more painful and realistic memories of Bruce's rapid deterioration as the cancer took hold.

The man who left the doctor's surgery that day was a different person from the man who had entered it earlier .How could it be otherwise having been the recipient of such grim news?

Mutterings from the chemo chair

{Or emotional reactions to other peoples' good intentions}

"Oh, aren't you looking well …. so much better than the last time I saw you."

Tooth grinding stuff, said with the best of intentions, but phrases that invoke a surge of annoyance in me and I feel my blood pressure soaring.

I grin an empty smile.

Have they really forgotten that is exactly what they said the last time we met? And the time before that; and on even earlier occasions. Begs the question, does it not, as to how, exactly, did I look three or four visits ago?

Anyway, there is a presumption present – that since I look relatively fit and able, which I do, there must have been some improvement in my condition. Lucky me.

But actually I feel pretty lousy and not in the least able to cope with the traditional niceties of polite conversation however well intentioned that might turn out to be. I am not feeling sorry for myself, or even ill for that matter, just totally unable to cope with exertion, decision making or anything more than a monosyllabic conversation. I am just incredibly weary, occasionally prone to narcolepsy, and somehow I feel detached from the realities of life. In this state all I want to do is rest and sleep, not entertain or be entertained by well meaning and caring friends or relatives.

But this is a self-centred and self-protective mode that I am in, albeit drug induced, and I know that, so I do my best to be positive and chatty and forthcoming with the folk who have come to visit and who are now somewhat uncertain how to deal with me. Do we mention cancer? Do we ask about treatment and its effects? Do we show an interest in his condition? Or do we just ignore it altogether and pretend nothing is different?

I don't mind either way, actually

But I do so wish that well used opening gambit were less frequently invoked. Much rather nothing said or, at best, 'good to see you' … or some such other platitude.

More mutterings from the chemo chair

[Or conversation with my cancer]

"Well, hello there, stranger". Except that now you are no stranger. Then neither are you a friend.

"What am I?" do you say.

"How about an interloper … you know, an unwelcome visitor? Oh, come now, of course you're not welcome, even on a temporary basis. You have interrupted my life style, corrupted my being, caused my family and me much havoc both mentally and physically and you expect me to embrace you with tolerance and understanding. Get lost! I really do not have time to deal with you at all, let alone just now.

What's that? Have you not been of *any* benefit to me? I suppose the answer to that question would depend on what you class as a benefit. Physically certainly not, mentally I do not accept your existence and I resist your presence on both fronts.

Thus to acknowledge any positive effects you may have had is somewhat of an anathema that is difficult for me to deal with, but I suppose if I am to be truthful – and why should I be so to you? – you have brought me an heightened awareness of my own mortality which prior to your invasion did not seriously colour my thinking or lifestyle. Now I am more aware of the sands of time and the need to embrace life more fully than perhaps I did.

Indeed, you have been the root cause of my meeting some delightful people, folk that I would not otherwise have met and that certainly is a bonus as is the recently acquired realisation just how compassionate, caring and loving other people can be. Day by day the cynic in me is being dissolved and melted, not only by caring nurses and hospital staff, but by sympathetic volunteers, concerned friends, fellow patients and a tolerant, loving wife.

I am indeed blessed and I shall not permit even your grey shadow to blight such good fortune.

Begone, dull care; there is no place for you in my life.

Further mutterings from the Chemo Chair

(Or, toxicity and its effects)

Interesting.

This process of poisoning my body. Or rather, having my body poisoned It's all done so charmingly and caringly that it's almost a pleasure to look forward to … and I'm not a masochist at heart or by inclination.

Drip, trickle; drip trickle, the steady monotony of the drug slipping into the vein of my hand whilst I doze, or read, or think of other things carries with it a certain hypnosis that the busy surrounding atmosphere does nothing to dispel. Nurses bustle and chatter. In the other six reclining chairs my companion patients exchange stories and life-style details yet the room and the treatment manage to relax and envelope me in a strange kind of calm.

But perhaps efficiency and courtesy are something to do with the way I feel. Confidence in my handlers, so to speak, plays its part in no uncertain fashion and there is little doubt in my mind that the nurses staffing this unit must have been handpicked and trained. They exude cheeriness, confidence and knowledge and seem able to relax every fresh patient that arrives.

But for now this two hour break does give me time to consider the after effects of the chemotherapy treatment. There is, as they say, 'no such thing as a free lunch'…. but I have been fortunate. None of the painful bones or joints and yellowing skin and only a bare modicum of the terrible sickness attacks. However, hair loss was quick in coming, far sooner than I had somehow anticipated. But that was not a great problem for me and I found that complete baldness was just another item to deal with along with the increase in body chill factor occasioned by my lack of hair.

Far more bothersome was the incredible weariness that invaded my being, the breaking of teeth, the mouth ulcers that suddenly blossomed and the disintegrating finger and toe nails. These began to split, chip and dissolve. 'Onycholysis', said my Consultant 'You're one of the 5% or so to get it…' 'That's not much relief', I grumbled to myself from the retrospective comfort of the chemo chair, forgetting for a while just how lucky I was being in getting off so lightly and abruptly becoming aware that I had completely neglected to discuss with him the occasional strong bouts of 'pins and needles' in my feet. These attacks invariably created a numbness and lack of sensation, so much so that I would be unable to drive our car. I would have no idea of the location of the pedal I was endeavouring to utilise.

But all of this musing was brought into focus and reality as the pump beside me buzzed into life to draw attention to the fact that my dosage had been completed and I knew that this session was finished.

So, until next time, which will be my tenth and last in this round of treatment, I am sure that ` my `chair will meet many more occupants. I hope they do as well as I appear to be managing yet I cannot help but ponder on the likelihood of my needing to face up to other side effects that may be still to come my way and of which l am presently unaware.

Final mutterings from the Chemo Chair

{Music Hall jokes and other contemplations]

There's an odd resonance to that word 'final'. I'm not yet ready for too much finality in my life, but for the present there will be no further mutterings from the chemo chair since this particular round of therapy is now coming to its end and this is my last session.

'So what comes next?' I ask myself.

There was never any question of my cancer being eradicated by the chemotherapy; it is a matter of whether or not the treatment I have had has been enough to stem its further advance. Time will tell, but if I have learnt anything from contracting cancer it is, perhaps, to expect the unexpected, so it appears to be a matter of wait and see. None of the medical profession with whom I am in contact are prepared to give me any prognosis and the phrase 'everyone reacts differently' has been so frequently spoken during the previous six months of treatment that it carries the air of a very well used, but no longer funny, music hall joke.

I know that the phrase illustrates a truth, but I find it to be of little help when considering my own particular situation.

I wriggle in the chair and make sure that I have not disconnected the umbilical connection that runs between the pump and the back of my hand. Morosely I watch the docataxel trickle into my vein. Heigh ho – not too long to go now and I cannot decide whether I should be pleased or resigned at the completion of this particular course of medication. I've heard that each sachet of the drug costs around £500 and my mind has difficulty in grappling with this figure. Ten sachets have been used during my visits and without the NHS this would have been an unaffordable treatment for me to undertake. Let's hope that for this sort of money there is some degree of success at the end of the day.

On reflection I have come to the realisation that the whole of the chemotherapy process has been far less intimidating than I had originally supposed it might be. I'm not quite sure what it was I had anticipated, if anything, but for me the reality turned out to be quite simple and painless, if somewhat time consuming. Two hours of consultation and medical attention has not once been completed in less than double that amount of time – on some occasions, considerably longer - so I learnt early on not to make any other arrangements on "chemo" days. But that has been a small price to pay and I have had no difficulty in filling the waiting times, aided by a comfortable, if busy, waiting area well supplied with literature, and some very attentive volunteers whose aim in life appears to be to supply one with endless cups of liquid refreshment and the occasional biscuit.

On the other hand, despite studying leaflets, talking to doctors and consultants and generally endeavouring to acquire as much information as possible, I have been taken unawares by some of the effects I have experienced in the wake of my treatment. Some of these I have noted in my earlier "mutterings." However, on further contemplation I have come to appreciate that my own lack of medical knowledge brings its own difficulties. I do not always know the right questions to ask or, if I do, in all innocence I interpret the given reply incorrectly.

Again, because cancer is not my sole medical irregularity (and the onset of old age plays its part too), when unusual problems arise I am not sure whether I should be contacting oncology, cardiology or my own GP.

With a drug induced state of mind that keeps me tired and indecisive I have been and do find these aspects of my illness stressful and difficult to handle.

Nevertheless, I have survived and coped with the effects of six months of chemotherapy – as have others near and dear to me. I have come to realise that those with whom I have been in regular and close contact have also suffered with me, perhaps not physically but certainly emotionally and mentally. Dealing with an unwell, curmudgeonly, irritable, sleep-deprived person is not the easiest and most appealing of pastimes.

But then neither is playing host to a cancer ....

Mind Games

'Tis a long road,
a dark and winding road,
that, in the middle of a Winter's eve
finds the recesses of my mind
and brings to the memory tales of
The Ghouls that haunt the fields,
The Gremlins lurking 'mid the rocks
and the wicked Trolls that dwell
and hide beneath every bridge
or behind the largest trees.

A moaning wind clutches at these trees,
bending them, creaking their trunks.
Or is there a Griffin at large
ponderously stalking me
and I am mis-reading sounds?
A hazy, cloud ridden moon
does little to light my way
and bring some relief
to the rapidly coalescing fears
that are gathering in my being.

A shape takes form before me.
A surge of panic paralyses me
before the hooting owl swoops on his way
impervious to my anxieties.
But now I am apprehensive –
disquiet and unease invade my mind
clawing at my struggling calm.
And these burgeoning, primeval instincts
bid me speed up and dally not.

Yet hist! A rustle in the hedgerow
and my tautened nerves quiver
before nervousness
slides inexorably into a fear.
that keeps me rooted to the spot.
Has the monstrous Kraken arisen
from the deep to pursue me?
Does some vampire seek my blood?
Fright galvanises me forward;
I break into a stumbling run.

Sweat blinds my eyes
and terror invades my soul.
I must flee before I am consumed
by the Four Horsemen I hear pounding
behind me on this loathsome way
that is my one avenue of escape.
Forward, ever forward. With speed.
The undead are tramping behind
and I am frightened beyond belief..
Is there no end, no exit?

Not whilst paranoia exists.

Ooch, It's Gie Dreich

That it is; on all fronts, it would appear.

Dare one say 'depression hovers', since that is how it seems? But then, perhaps, weatherwise it does exactly that because the sky is grey, clouds are scudding frenziedly from horizon to horizon, the skeletal trees sway in the gusting wind and falling rain glistens and glides on roof tiles close by.

The weather complements the mood and the thoughts that skitter through a lack-lustre mind, one that today is being succoured by a brain that gloomily dissects the world and its myriad occupants. Some times it is difficult to drag one's thoughts away from a negative approach to events, things and people, as hard as one might try so to do. Today is one such day and the weather reflects my own ineffectual struggle to lighten the mood.

Dreich is a good onomatopoeic Scots word, yet today it seems too insignificant a word for the occasion, the weather and the all pervading doldrums.

Yeah. Oh, yeah. Depression reigns supreme …… and what shall we do?

How It Is

I wallow,
surveying the Christmas cards
that are to be written
and sent.

The season of Goodwill and Love
is upon us.
But who are these people,
once met.
barely known,
long gone
who now require remembrance?

They bear no kinship
to the child
born in a stable far away
and long ago.

Instead,
They are passing strangers,
Christian people, perhaps,
But prey to the lights,
Candles and presents,
With faint recollection of times past.

Now,
who is next on the list?

Portents

Alert and proud
she stands,
surveying her world
with Confidence and Assurity
that say,
I WILL be Alpha Dog.

Not yet fully grown
{but a stage from puppyhood},
all the impish traits
of doggy teenager-hood
are evident in her beauty, power
and governance
I WILL be Alpha Dog.

And in that early time
she learns from her elders
as her physique strengthens.
She gnaws her bone,
guards her bed jealously
and dependent months pass by.
I WILL be Alpha Dog.

So look to her
you who are older
and wiser.
She is strong, She is here,
Her time is coming.
She WILL be Alpha Dog.

A Lamentation for Samantha

When delving through a dusty box, I found this snap of you.
amongst the many photographs of those I loved and knew;
a picture taken long time ago when you were in your prime
at a moment when I did not know how swiftly passed the time.
still left for me to share your life before your fateful end
came all too soon, depriving me of a close, beloved friend.
For knowing you enriched my soul in a manner once unknown.
and now my days are emptier, just knowing that you've gone,
though time cannot erase the thoughts that dwell within my mind
the tender , pleasant memories that you have left behind
which, happily, surmount the pain your leaving left with me,
but, oh, I wish that you were here and sitting at my knee.

For you were once my Alpha dog, so bold and strong and true,
the leader of a motley pack that chased and stalked and knew
each path and track and rabbit hole that dotted field and moor.
A pack that followed steadfastly when once you found a spoor
until you tired of such games and then would homeward flee.

to take your place, in regal style, upon the old settee
Where you could rest in comfort whilst you watched my every move
in case I ventured out of sight – of which you disapproved.
From birth you had decided that your place was at my side
and ever were you with me, escort, workmate, minder, guide;
e'en now when years have split us, I recall you oft and well
and tears do fall more frequently than I would care to tell
.
For though I mourn my vanished friend, the brown-eyed golden bitch
whose presence captivated me and made my life so rich,
there are so many memories of merriment and fun
when you were young and impish as we frolicked in the sun.
Or later , when you quietly gave birth to all your pups
and never thought to protest when I dared to pick them up.
So in my mind there is no doubt you were a people dog,
of this there is no question and I will not pettifog
for oft I watched you welcome folk in open, joyful style,
Allowing them to stroke your head, pay homage for a while.
Yet I believe, within my heart, I was your closest friend
and ne'er shall I forgive the man who sent you to your end.

For had I closed the gate that day and kept you here with me,
had I observed you running off so fast and boisterously

ahead your pack, to search the moor and flush out grouse
and hare,
to lope your way ’cross nearby fields to find the fox’s lair
or comb the hedgerows hunting pheasant nestled the
verge,
had I seen you, called you back and stemmed that
hunting urge,
Things would have turned or differently and change there
would have been
you would have played a different role in quite another
scene.
But, ah, dear Sam, ‘twas not be that sad, unwelcome day.
Instead you found a poacher’s trap which stopped you on
your way.
So snared and held, for sure in pain, you came not home
that night
And I grew very worried as the darkness turned to light.

As dawn arrived, the sun awoke and you came not back
to me,
I set off in an anxious hunt, just searching desperately
and listening for a sound or bark, but sadly hearing
nought,
then slowly realising that you had been killed or caught.
But nonetheless I persevered for many a fruitless hour
Through woods and fields, in croft and barn,the country
did I scour.
All through that morn your erstwhile pack did drift home
one by one,
but of my lovely Alpha bitch, good news there came but
none.
With spirits low I watched the gate and prayed for your
return.
As day wore on and eve approached, I grew quite
taciturn

and restless, angry, fractious, grieved, I set off yet again
once more to comb the fields and hedge and copse and
ditch and lane.

But still it was I did not find the slightest trace of you
and wearily I turned back home, despondent, sad and
blue.
For then I knew, within my heart, some awful thing had
chanced
to keep you back as night came down and all my fears
enhanced.
How slow in passing is the night when one just cannot
sleep,
when vivid thoughts attack the mind and one is prone to
weep,
when trying to be rational is but a waste of time
and useless are the plans that form , devoid of sense or
rhyme.
Thus passed that second, lonely night so full of tears and
stress,
but how much worse were your long hours I cannot start
to guess
for captured, held in painful grip from which there was
no flight
There was so little you could do to ease your awful
plight.

But some time later on that day a person found you there
Was it the poacher who returned and freed you from the
snare?
Or someone else who tramped the fields and liberated
you?
'Though time has passed, the puzzle stays; oh, how I
wish I knew

what happened on that sunny day before the ,phone rang here,
for neighbours kind had found you, stretched out prone but, oh, so near.
Weary, bloodstained, almost home, you greeted me with joy –
I had no mind to scold you, my straying, blonde tomboy
Although, in truth, my heart just sank to see your sorry state
And I could not help but ponder as to what might be your fate.
So I took you in my arms and I endeavoured not to fret
As I brought you home, dressed your wound and telephoned the vet.

The surgery, they took you in and placed you on a drip.
They x-rayed, bathed and bound your leg from foot up to the hip.
I felt so very angry as I brought you home again
and I cursed the callous person who had caused you so much pain.
But all my cursing, all my care, were useless in the end
for your leg began to fester and the wound refused to mend
'til came that awful, wretched time I never shall forget
when like some over-ripened fruit your leg began to blet
as gangrene attacked the limb despite my utmost care
and knowledge that your death loomed close was more than I could bear,
for though I fought to stem and clear the poison's deadly flow,
'twas in the end I lost the fight and I had to let you go.

Though time has passed and years have flown, this photograph of you
brings to mind the times we shared, the things we used to do.
You were so sure, companion bold, your place was at my side
and always did you match my mood with aptitude and pride.
Yet still, somehow, you kept your place ahead the motley pack
for none there was dare challenge you, or make some sly
attack upon your haughty presence which just emanated style
and hid an inborn toughness 'neath an aura quite docile.
Now, as I hold this photograph, I cannot exorcise
the memories that flood my mind, the tears that fill my eyes.
I miss, you, my Samantha, and the loss is hard to bear –
I live in hope we'll meet again, some time, some place, somewhere.

Pienza At Noon

A wasp buzzes inquisitively
around my glass of campari.

I watch a tangle of tour guides
as they chatter and joke
and laugh loudly.
They hustle and bustle
on the steps of The Duomo
whilst the sun heats the piazza
and bounces off marbled tiles.
The tourists meander,
gaze and ponder,
perspiring
'neath clear sky warmth.
This is mid-day Pienza.

And where best to lunch
Is a dilemma.

By San Cipriano lake

Undulating purple mountains
peer protectively
over the deciduous forest
which is their blanket,
sweeping in profuse abandonment
down to water's edge
where the sun shimmers
a pathway to the horizon.

And a distant dog barks.

Graceful, sedate and watchful
the cruising swans prowl,
paddling slowly among rising fish
whose leap-created splashes
jeer exuberantly at the aged angler
as he casts yet again,
still without luck.
No dinner tonight.

Now the impish wind
creates runnels of water,
spearheads dancing and arrowing
across the lake's surface
as they race to oblivion.
Then the capricious breeze softens,
gives lift to the gliding hunter
who sweeps past on outstretched wings.

In a silent, seeking search he patrols
the woods, the water,
the scattered beaches
that are spaces between trees.
But he, like the angler,
is not rewarded
and the quiet beauty around
is no compensation for either.

But later the breeze grows lazy.
Strength oozes from the sun
and the lake's bright roadway
narrows to a shrivelled glimmer.
Now darting swallows
replace the gracious swans.
Rustling trees. Purple hills.
Green waters and tranquillity abound.

Until a distant dog barks.

Lady in Grey

Companion for an hour,
who are you?
Did you enjoy our meeting
as much as I?

Lonely, middle-aged woman,
transitory, educated,
a one night stand in the making?
Could be.
But no.
Just company and conversation
before Livorno beckoned.

Travelling Business Woman
I learned much,
but not enough.
For just an hour
in the Great Circle of Life
our paths met and touched
and I would fain
have spent more time in your company.

I wonder,
what is your name?

Ponderings

Where are they now, those one time friends,
and lovers, too, who through the years
I met and touched and passed and left
to go their ways with all their tears?
Their memories, etched upon my mind,
part mould and shape and bring remorse,
and ghosts that reach out from behind
sometimes do influence my course

And they, who've gone their different ways,
I wonder, have they part of me
that now and then in later days
they look on as a memory
which, when recalled, brings happiness,
not tears and sadness with the thought;
or do they think of me the less
and go their ways just as they ought?

If At First You Don't Succeed, Try, Try Again.

(Was Aesop correct?)

The little bird was safe in its nest halfway up the cliff side.

Over weeks, well fed by its parents who disappeared every morning to catch fish and subsequently returned later in the day – or even in the evening – to regurgitate their catch and feed their offspring, the little bird grew.

And grew.

And grew.

Until it became a healthy young fledgling at which stage it began to stretch and flap its wings.

Now it had the urge, but not yet the confidence, to fly as its parents did. Understanding this, the adults began to perch on nearby crags, calling and encouraging their offspring to join them.

Day after day the fledgeling flapped and exercised his wings and muscles. For many hours it did this, but still did not build up enough confidence to leave the nest.

Until, on the seventh day an updrift of air over the cliff abruptly caught the flapping bird and lifted it from its perch on the edge of the nest.

'I can fly', thought the bird, but it lacked experience and plummeted down the cliff face to the sea below. There it instinctively tried to flap its way into the air once more as its parents circled, calling urgently from above.

But it had not yet developed the expertise to carry out this manoeuvre and the waiting shark had an easy meal.

Moral: Sometimes it is wiser to give up rather than continue trying.

Never Say 'Boo' to a Goose

"He wouldn't say 'Boo' to a goose", they said;
I'll show them I'm not soft in the head!
I went to my Auntie's farm after tea,
I hid by the goose hut and counted to three.
I'd made my plan – I knew what to do,
I plucked up the courage and then shouted
"BOO".

Well! I wasn't prepared for what happened then.
He jumped right off the ground and came down on a hen
And the hen squawked so loudly it woke up the pig –
I've never seen a pig quite as BIG!
She started to chase me, all through the mud,
So I slipped and fell with a gi-normous THUD
In the midst of a rose bush all covered in thorns.
The next thing I saw was a huge pair of HORNS.
The goat had joined in since it looked like such fun
Chasing 'the boy' in the hot Summer sun;
'The boy' was me and I was confused,
Which way should I run?

And BOY, was I bruised.

I got out of the rose bush and made for the wall
And the next thing I heard was a loud CATERWAUL!
I had stepped on the cat with my big, clumsy feet.
OK! I surrender! I admit to defeat!
The animals cheered and then set me loose.
Never, NEVER, say 'Boo' to a goose.

(A poem by my daughter-in-law Nicola Beveridge. It arrived with a request for a reply …)

Never Say 'Boo' to a Goose
(A reprise from Ovaltine the pig)

That meddling young boy, that daft 'townie' child,
Does he not know that he's driving us wild
With his noise and his capers, his games and his antics,
The whole farm is swiftly becoming quite frantic?
He's chasing the hens and pursuing the ducks
(If he tries that with me … he'll be right out of luck),
Just look at him now as he hides by that bush
What on earth is he up to? Shall I give him a push?
I think not … not now, I'm enjoying this mire,
The mud is quite heavenly and I'm really quite tired.

Good Heavens; how silly to yell at the goose,
If he has any sense he will quickly vamoose
Before he's assaulted and nastily bitten,
Say 'Boo' to a goose, in lore it is written,
And disappear fast whilst you still have the chance
For an unhappy goose will attack and advance.
But what a kerfuffle; oh, drat, what a din,
That 'Boo' has awakened my farm kith and kin;
There's squawking, and baa-ing, and moos from the cow,
I'll have to get up, put an end to this row.

Oh, what a laugh we've all had
As we took a farmyard revenge on the lad.
I chased him first, all through the mud,
'Til he fell on his face with a glorious thud.
Then Gertie the goat picked him up with her horns
And tossed him right into a rose bush with thorns.
He struggled to his feet with a yelp and a squeal
And set off a-running with our dogs at his heels.
All flustered and bothered he jumped o'er the wall –
There was a screeching 'miaow' as the cat broke his fall.

His big clumsy feet had caught the cat’s tail
And the feline shot off with a loud, piercing wail
To leap on the wall with a mew and a hiss
As everyone gathered to savour the bliss
Of the moment – the foe had been routed.
Then the lad reached his feet and tearfully shouted,
“I’m sorry. I’m sorry.” He called with a moan,
“I’ll really be good if you leave me alone.”
So we all cheered aloud and we let him go loose
Knowing he’d never again ‘Boo’ a goose.

The Dancer In the Trees

Red spirit dancing through the trees,
you scamper, leap with practised ease,
the essence of bright summer days
encaptured in your playful ways
brings joy and wonder to my soul –
oh, how I mourn your passing role.

Now that your cousin sweeps the land
and all the forests you once spanned
have ceased to be your sole domain –
your loss the grey invader's gain –
how precious are these moments rare
when you can frolic without care.

And so, entranced, I stand and gaze
and watch you dance among the maze
of trunks and branches, boughs and leaves,
a Will O' The Wisp high in the trees;
I hope I never see the day
when you depart your Highland drey.

Earthbound

If there's regret within my soul
It's all to do with thee;
I hear the stirring, urgent calls
As you fly over me
And, at that sound, I am transfixed
By urges deep and strong
That bid me leave all earthly things
And join your winging throng.

Wild geese, wild geese I watch you pass
In shifting, ordered dance
And all the while your cries ring clear,
Your numbers to enhance.
So skeins close ranks, the numbers swell,
The spearheads tighten form
Just arrowing across the sky
In squadrons aliform.

Whilst I stand still, earthbound and sad
That I cannot join your flight
And go with you to far off lands
Where sun's rays conquer night.
Yet nonetheless my spirit flies
Aloft in joyous glee
In answer to your haunting calls
That ever summon me.

The Winter Gloaming

Grey clouds framed by a golden sky,
which shades to palest blue,
Hold promise of more snow foreby
to cloak the trees anew.
The gloaming, clear and cold and still
becalms a Winter's day
and frames the sheep upon the hill
as they flock 'round bales of hay
fresh spread by calloused, frozen hands
with fingertips so numb –
The Farmer, cursing snowbound land
as he longs for Springtime sun.
Yet as he craves for days to come
and yearns his life away,
the gloaming darkens into night
'til stars and frost hold sway.

The Bracken on the Brae

The bracken moved upon the brae
That sad and well remembered day
As you thrust past without a care
Intent on scents that filled the air.
A hunting buzzard circled high,
Just wheeling in an azure sky
Above the burn, the pines, the gorse,
The drover's path, the river's course
The rocky bank you knew so well
That day you bade those sights farewell.

Yet young again, with jaunty stance,
You stopped your trotting with a glance
At howling jets that thundered then
Along the quiet, sunbathed glen
And, as the flypast skimmed from view,
You shook yourself, took off anew,
With old times vigour that belied
The creeping illness deep inside
That caught you at your very best
When you were lithe and full of zest.

At river's edge you drank your fill
And then you headed for the hill
Where hare would race and deer would roam
And rabbits burrowed deep their homes,
But slope and scrub and fallen trees
Made going hard across the scree
And where you once would run and stalk
You soon began to pant and walk.
With heavy heart I watched you so,
Your fitness gone, now ill and slow.

If there was pain, you bore it well,
Succumbing to the deadly spell
With braveness and such gentle calm;
Too late, I learned you'd come to harm.
'Twas later still your ravaged shape
Showed all the signs of cancer's rape-
The lumps, the scabs, the falling hair,
Your sad, sad eyes and listless air.
I knew then. deep within my heart,
That the time had come for us to part.

I called you close and stroked your head,
Remembering the years we'd shared.
Oh, how I'll miss your morning howl,
Your bark and your protective growl.
No more the days when we will stride
Through forest, stream and countryside.
In angriness I spilled my grief,
But cursing loud brought no relief
And the lovely glen through which we strolled
So suddenly seemed drear and cold.

Slowly we retraced our path,
This time not back to home and hearth,
Subdued companions side by side
To take that last unwelcome ride.
A final romp, as was your habit,
Seeking some unwary rabbit,
Squirrel, badger, mouse or vole,
Investigating every hole
'Til heaving, gasping for each breath,
You joined the car … and rode to death.

A shaven leg, the needle's prick,
To end your life was sure and quick.
I held you, lifeless and inert,
And sobbed my grief, my loss, my hurt.
But spirit lives, 'though flesh may die,
Your presence is so often nigh,
Because your daughter walks with me
And brings to mind the used-to-be,
The more so when she thrusts her way
Among the bracken on the brae.

The Hoodie

Stop. Look. Regard the hooded crow
Surveying all the word below
From perch up there on branch so high
He watches with a piercing eye.
A scavenger with mien so bold,
A fearsome foe, or so it's told,
To birthing sheep and new born lambs,
To eggs and oysters, mussels, clams.
Alone he sits there, quiet and still,
Now preening with that wicked bill
Ere he decides which way to go –
To fly, or strut the ground below.
Yet in repose, a handsome chap
Whose plumage mixes grey with black
As now he spreads his wings to fly,
The preening done. His caw a cry
To split he air, tell kin and foes,
"I come, the King of all the crows".

Step Into the Evening

Pause.
Consideration.
Realisation.
I don't need to –
Step into the evening, I mean –
'cos I'm already there.

I have wandered into that gloaming
without curiosity,
without fear of the fading light,
without due awareness
and it has been my mortal frame
that has brought cognizance.

Now, from the twilight,
I consider the vanished day
and wonder if I made the best use
of its' passing.
Whether or not I did so
I cannot now step back.

A sigh waiting to happen

A groan as any other name
A sigh might be described
If sadness is within the frame
Of feelings not denied.

For why should sighing be of love
Or passions deeply known –
Do dreams of power or aims in life
Not rouse a breathy tone?

In some they do, in others not,
They, in their turn, reserve
Each uttered breath for moments sweet
Which only they observe.

Yet be it uttered, be it still,
The sigh constrained might be,
'Til bursting forth the sound is heard
As gasp or moan or plea.

And even at the close of Life
The sigh might be perceived
Just trickling from a dying soul
And Mourners know to grieve.

Requiem

Do not unduly weep for me
Now that I have passed from view
For I have left all Earthly things
To move to pastures new.
Unheard, unseen by mortal eye,
'Tis there I'll wait for thee
For I know that these Elysian Fields
Exist eternally.

Your world may be a darker place,
But waste not time in sorrow;
Let not sadness cloud your life,
Look forward to a brighter morrow
When we are once again as one,
Unchanged throughout the years,
United, loving, lovers, friends
And there'll be no place for tears.

For now is but a fleeting phase –
Forever waits at hand,
Prepared to banish time and space,
To bring you to the lovely land
Where I await.